ULTIMATE MANGA
HOW TO DRAW
ACTION MANGA

Marc Powell and David Neal

PowerKiDS press

New York

WITH THANKS TO ODA, STEVE, AILIN, AND PAT

Published in 2016 by **The Rosen Publishing Group**
29 East 21st Street, New York, NY 10010

Text by Jack Hawkins
Edited by Jack Hawkins
Designed by Dynamo Ltd and Emma Randall
Cover design by Notion Design
Illustrations by Marc Powell and David Neal

Cataloging-in-Publication Data
Powell, Marc.
How to draw action manga / by Marc Powell and David Neal.
p. cm. — (Ultimate manga)
Includes index.
ISBN 978-1-4994-1138-6 (pbk.)
ISBN 978-1-4994-1147-8 (6 pack)
ISBN 978-1-4994-1167-6 (library binding)
1.Comic books, strips, etc. — Japan — Technique — Juvenile
literature. 2. Cartooning — Japan — Technique — Juvenile
literature. 3. Action in art — Juvenile literature. I. Title.
NC1764.5.J3 P694 2016
741.5'1—d23

Manufactured in the United States of America
CPSIA Compliance Information: Batch WS15PK: For Further Information
contact Rosen Publishing, New York, New York at 1-800-237-9932

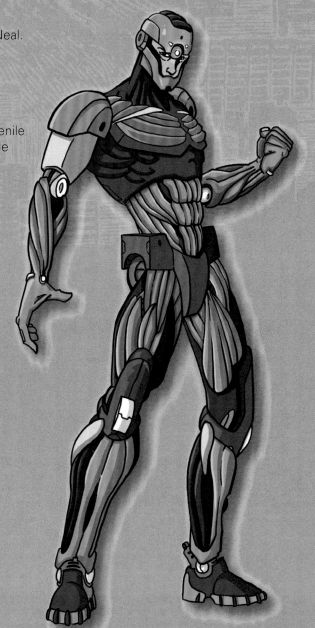

CONTENTS

HOW TO USE THIS BOOK

The drawings in this book have been built up in seven stages. Each stage uses lines of a different color so you can see the new layer clearly. Of course, you don't have to use different colors in your work. Use a pencil for the first four stages so you can get your drawing right before moving on to the inking and coloring stages.

Stage 1: Green lines
This is the basic stick figure of your character.

Stage 2: Red lines
The next step is to flesh out the simple stick figure.

Stage 3: Blue lines
Then finish the basic shape and add in extra details.

Stage 4: Black lines
Add in clothes and any accessories.

Stage 5: Inks
The inking stage will give you a final line drawing.

Stage 6: Colors
"Flat" coloring uses lighter shades to set the base colors of your character.

Stage 7: Shading
Add shadows for light sources, and use darker colors to add depth to your character.

BASIC TOOLS

You don't need lots of complicated, expensive tools for your manga images – many of them are available from a good stationery shop. The others can be found in any art supplies store, or online.

PENCILS

These are probably the most important tool for any artist. It's important to find a type of pencil you are comfortable with, since you will be spending a lot of time using it.

Graphite

You will be accustomed to using graphite pencils – they are the familiar wood-encased "lead" pencils. They are available in a variety of densities from the softest, 9B, right up to the hardest, 9H. Hard pencils last longer and are less likely to smudge on the paper. Most artists use an HB (#2) pencil, which falls in the middle of the density scale.

Mechanical pencils

Also known as propelling pencils, these contain a length of lead that can be replaced. The leads are available in the same densities as graphite pencils. The great advantage of mechanical pencils over graphite is that you never have to sharpen them – you simply extend more lead as it wears down.

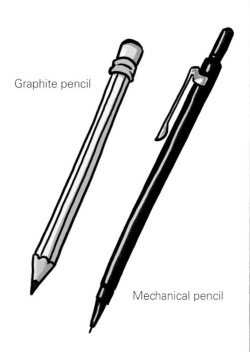

Graphite pencil

Mechanical pencil

Marker

Ballpoint pen

INKING PENS

After you have penciled your piece of artwork, you will need to ink the line to give a sharp, solid image.

Ballpoint pens

Standard ballpoint pens are ideal for lining your piece. However, their quality varies, as does their delivery of ink. A single good-quality ballpoint pen is better than a collection of cheap ones.

Marker pens

Standard marker pens of varying thicknesses are ideal for coloring and shading your artworks. They provide a steady, consistent supply of ink, and can be used to build layers of color by re-inking the same area. They are the tools most frequently used for manga coloring.

BIKER GANG LEADER

This tough character could be a hero or a villain. His dark clothing, hidden eyes, and clenched fist tell you he is dangerous to know. If his clothing isn't right for your story, you could dress him in something more old-fashioned or even futuristic.

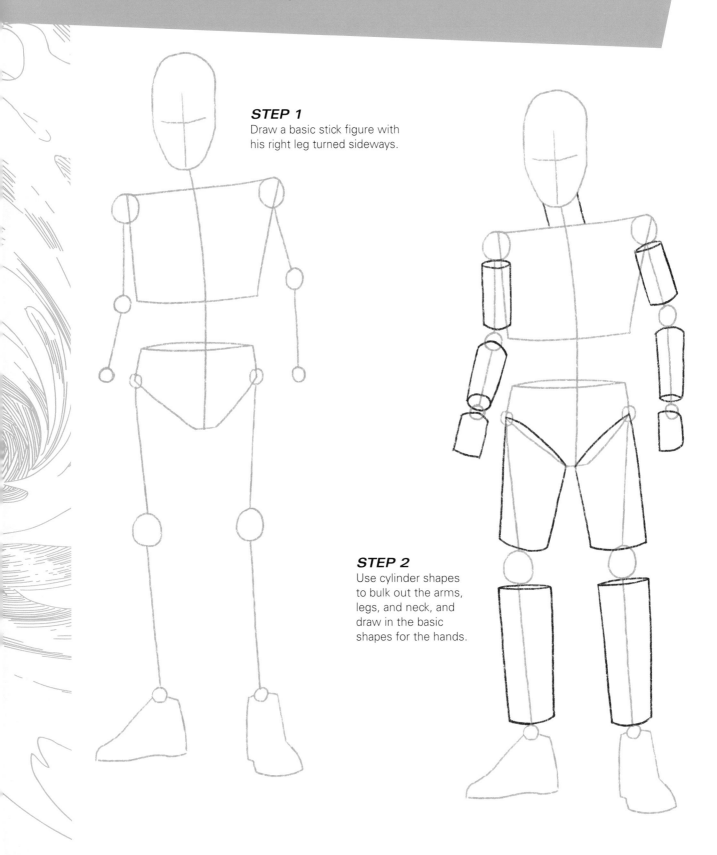

STEP 1
Draw a basic stick figure with his right leg turned sideways.

STEP 2
Use cylinder shapes to bulk out the arms, legs, and neck, and draw in the basic shapes for the hands.

STEP 3

Sketch in the anatomical details, including the extended fingers on the left hand and the closed right fist. Add the facial features. The eyes are hidden behind his goggles.

STEP 4

Draw the character's clothes and accessories, then draw his hair.

STEP 5

Use your lining pen to go over the lines that will be visible in the finished drawing. Add a shadow under the character's chin and mark the creases in his clothes. Then draw the chain hanging from his belt on the left. Erase any pencil lines.

STEP 6
Put in your basic flat colors as shown.

STEP 7
Add color to complete the shading and show the creases in the character's clothing.

KID HERO

Not all martial art fighters have to be powerful warriors with rippling muscles. Sometimes it's nice to mix things up a little by putting all that fighting power into a small, excitable package.

STEP 1

Draw a stick figure of a boy jumping in the air with his arms and legs outstretched. As he is young, his head is larger in proportion to his body than that of an adult. His pose means that his legs are foreshortened and the soles of his shoes are visible.

STEP 2

Use cylinder shapes to give bulk to his arms and legs and draw the basic shapes of his hands.

STEP 3
Sketch in your character's anatomical details, along with his facial features, fingers, and hair.

STEP 4
Add details to the facial features and give the boy some clothes and a necklace of large beads.

STEP 5

Use your lining pen to go over the lines that will be visible in the finished drawing. Add ragged edges to the sleeves and a twisted cord belt. Erase any pencil lines.

STEP 6
The graphic style of this character lends itself to the application of strong colors with hard edges for the base coloring.

STEP 7

Notice how the shadowing has a defined edge to match the graphic coloring style.

SPEED AND MOVEMENT

Action manga is all about turning ordinary life into something exciting. This can be done in a number of ways – the use of focus lines, perspective, and dynamic angles can all work together to turn the ordinary into the amazing.

This two-panel image of a car driving along a road could be used to show a character covering distance, but it just isn't exciting.

Now take a look at the panels on the left. Changing the angles of the car and the shape of the border boxes gives a lot more movement to the scene. We have also added focus lines to reinforce the sense of urgency.

A great tip is to use opposing angles to add even more action. The car slants at one angle while the horizon slants at an opposing angle. This is an excellent way to make the scene even more dynamic.

You can pose your characters to add action to a scene. Here, the viewpoint is of one of the people involved in a fight. This is called first-person view and it immediately gives your story lots of drama.

First, you will need to set up the scene showing which characters are fighting. Then you could switch to a first-person view. The use of perspective and foreshortening makes the fist look large and menacing. The punch leaps right off the page and towards the viewer. Watch out!

You could try basing your drawing on perspective lines. This takes a little more planning at the rough stage, but it is effective at showing the power and flow of a scene.

A triangle technique is used for the perspective lines. The leading foot shows the fighter is stepping forwards into the attack, while his leading fist is about to connect a punch. The use of perspective then leads your eye towards his trailing fist. This suggests that he will follow up the original attack with a strike upwards towards his opponent's head. Using perspective has allowed us to show the entire attack scene in a single panel.

CYBORG WARRIOR

Part human and part machine, this cyborg is always ready for its next mission. The ribbing on his metal body mimics the shape of real, flesh-and-blood muscles, emphasizing his strength and also his humanity. He's not just a robot!

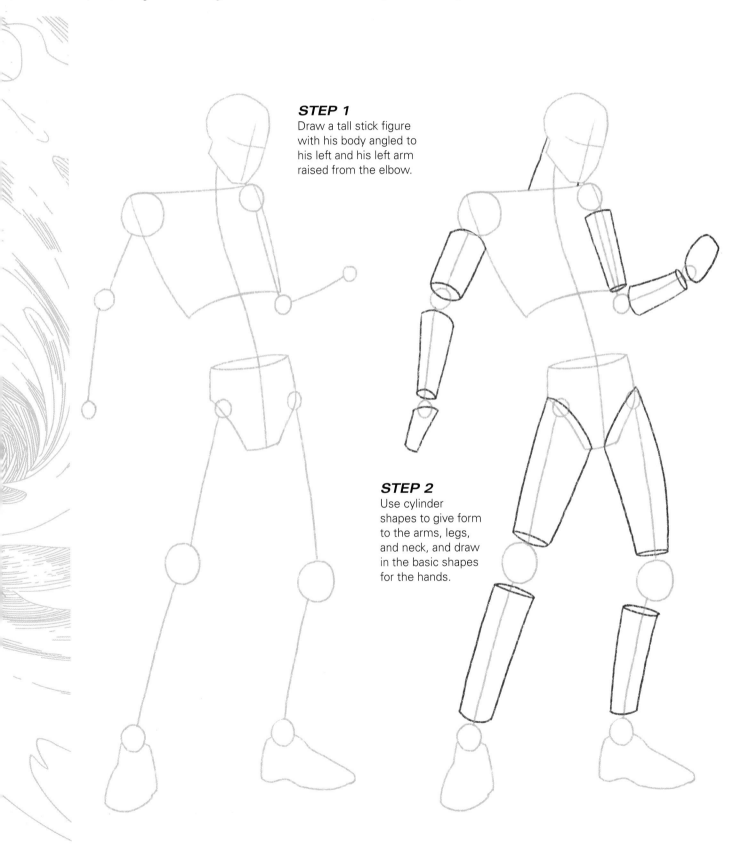

STEP 1
Draw a tall stick figure with his body angled to his left and his left arm raised from the elbow.

STEP 2
Use cylinder shapes to give form to the arms, legs, and neck, and draw in the basic shapes for the hands.

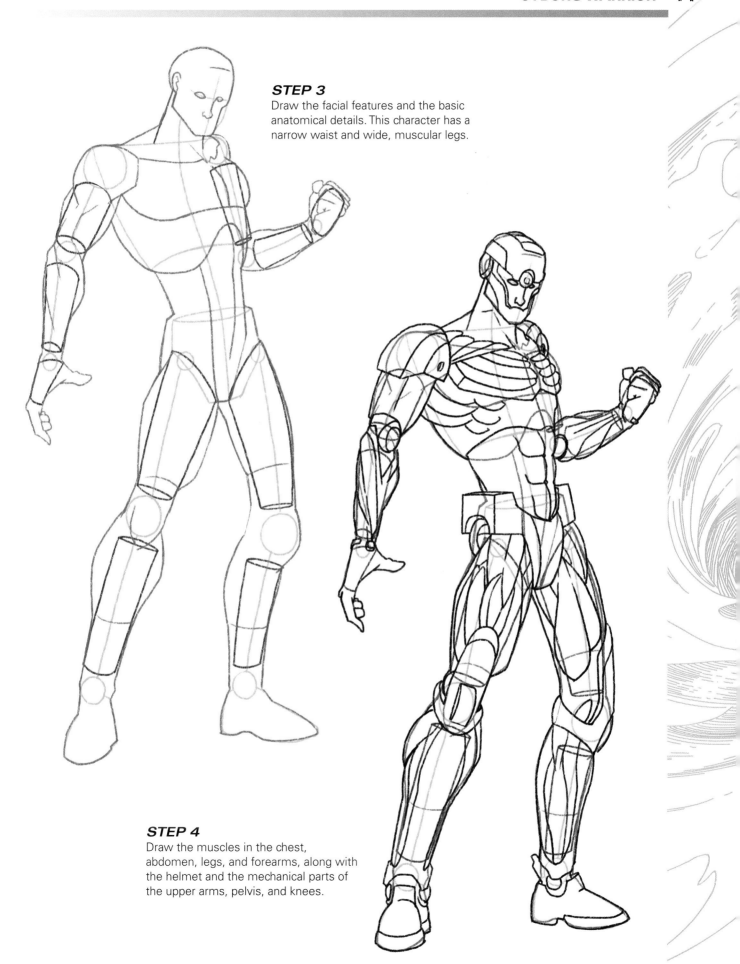

STEP 3
Draw the facial features and the basic anatomical details. This character has a narrow waist and wide, muscular legs.

STEP 4
Draw the muscles in the chest, abdomen, legs, and forearms, along with the helmet and the mechanical parts of the upper arms, pelvis, and knees.

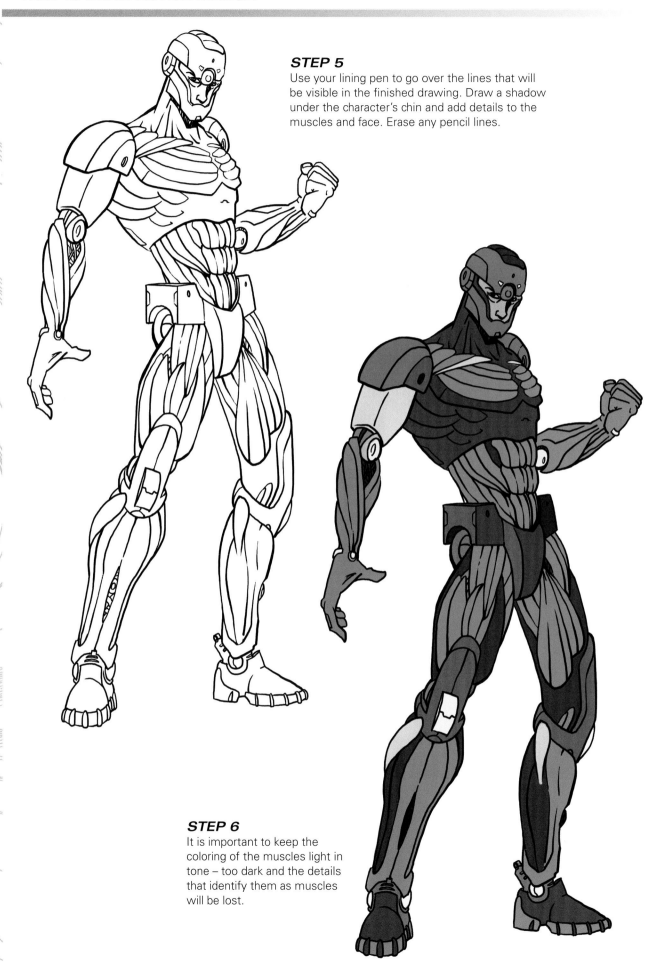

STEP 5
Use your lining pen to go over the lines that will be visible in the finished drawing. Draw a shadow under the character's chin and add details to the muscles and face. Erase any pencil lines.

STEP 6
It is important to keep the coloring of the muscles light in tone – too dark and the details that identify them as muscles will be lost.

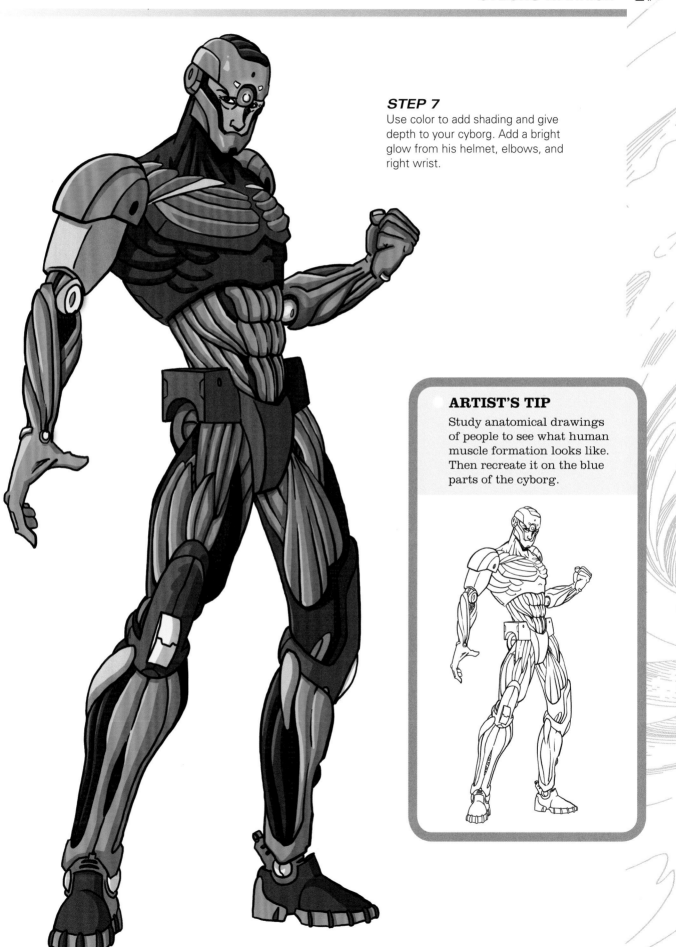

STEP 7

Use color to add shading and give depth to your cyborg. Add a bright glow from his helmet, elbows, and right wrist.

● ARTIST'S TIP

Study anatomical drawings of people to see what human muscle formation looks like. Then recreate it on the blue parts of the cyborg.

MUSCLE MAN

There are strong powerful men in almost every area of manga. You may meet them in fights or they may appear in the background, as bodyguards. There is always a place for the guy who looks as though he can lift a car with one hand.

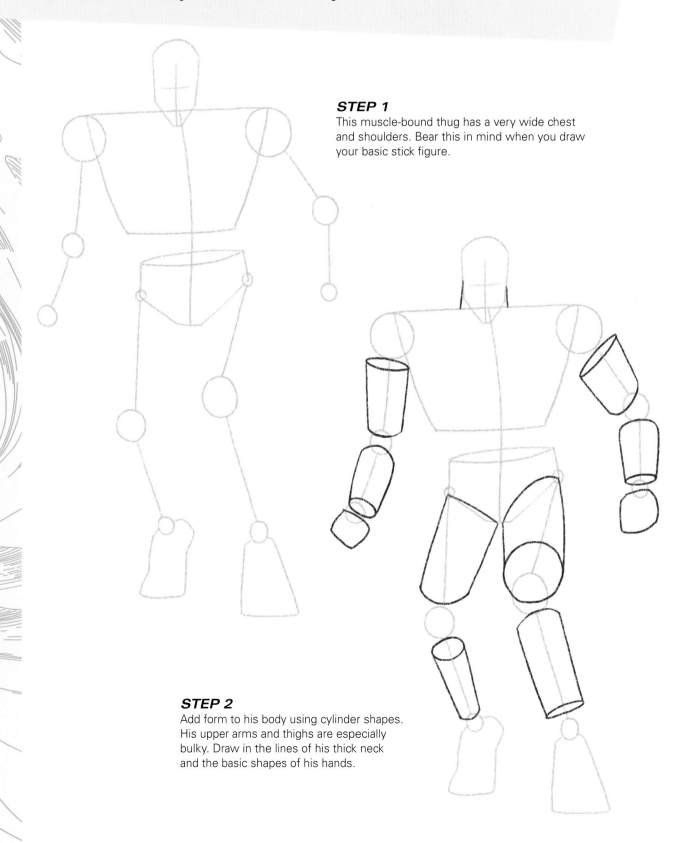

STEP 1
This muscle-bound thug has a very wide chest and shoulders. Bear this in mind when you draw your basic stick figure.

STEP 2
Add form to his body using cylinder shapes. His upper arms and thighs are especially bulky. Draw in the lines of his thick neck and the basic shapes of his hands.

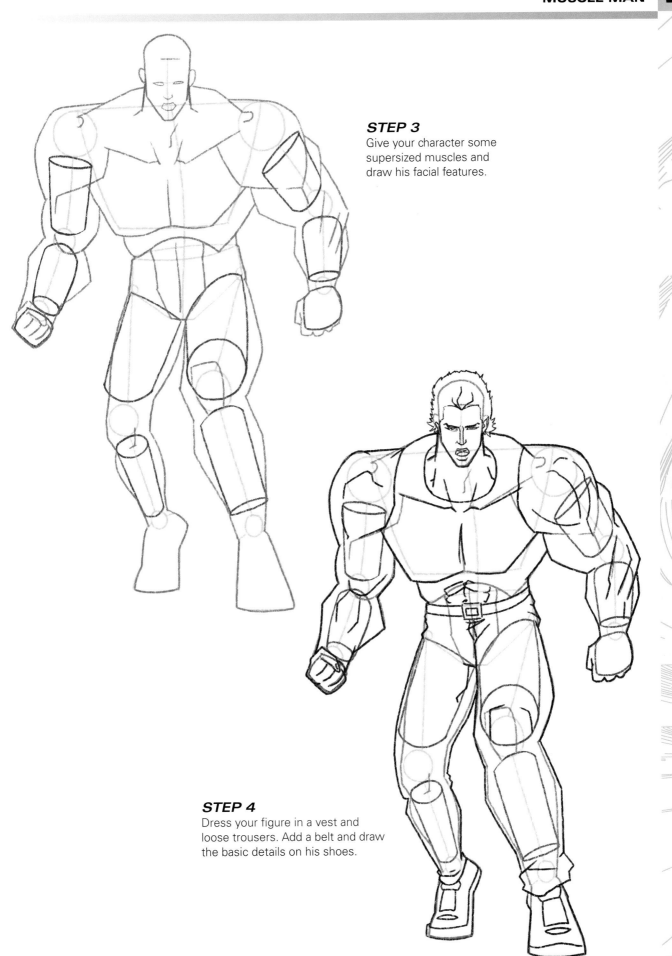

STEP 3
Give your character some
supersized muscles and
draw his facial features.

STEP 4
Dress your figure in a vest and
loose trousers. Add a belt and draw
the basic details on his shoes.

STEP 5

Use your lining pen to go over the lines that will be visible in the finished drawing. Add shading to define your character's muscles and show the creases in his pants. Complete the details in the shoes and facial features and add some hair. Erase any pencil lines.

STEP 6

Next, put in the base coloring. The dark shades used here give this big guy a threatening appearance.

STEP 7
Use darker colors to complete
the shading. This will give more
depth to your drawing.

STRIKE A POSE!

For artists, a stick figure is the starting point for any character drawing. It provides the basis for the character's form and pose. This stick figure is jointed and has a head, torso, and feet so that it resembles the human skeleton. By using this figure you will be able to pose your characters for any action, and still keep them looking natural and realistic.

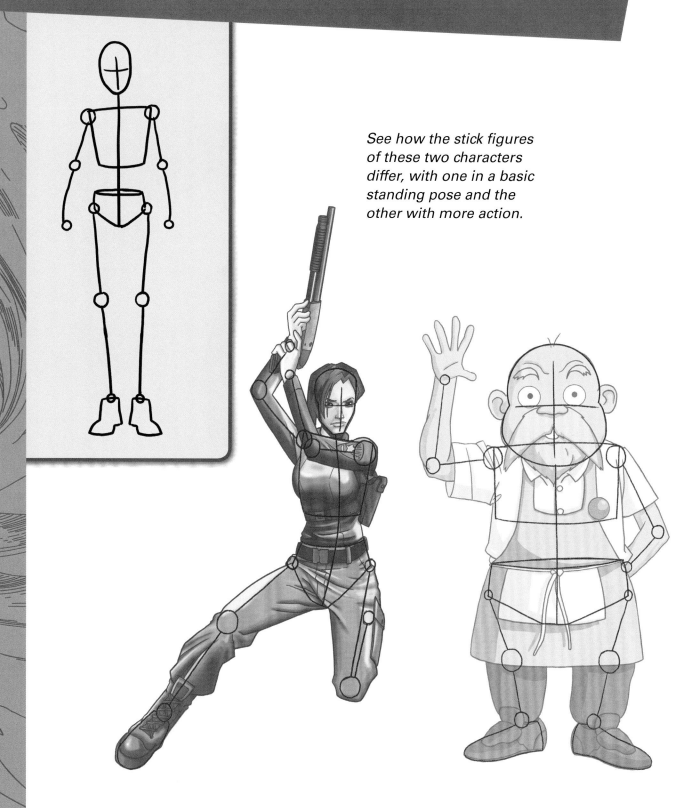

See how the stick figures of these two characters differ, with one in a basic standing pose and the other with more action.

Stick figures allow you to get your pose exactly how you want it. They enable you to make changes at the beginning so that you don't have to alter your fully fleshed-out drawing. Practice drawing stick figures in different poses until you feel comfortable doing them.

Walking

Running

Waving

Standing

Jumping

Crouching

Here are some basic poses. Once you have mastered these, try stick figures that are stretching, balancing, sitting, leaping, and climbing.

MASTER CRIMINAL

The very angular and pointed style of this criminal gives him an air of menace. Just looking at him, you can tell he doesn't say much, but he will carry out evil orders without a second thought. How will your heroes escape from this dangerous man?

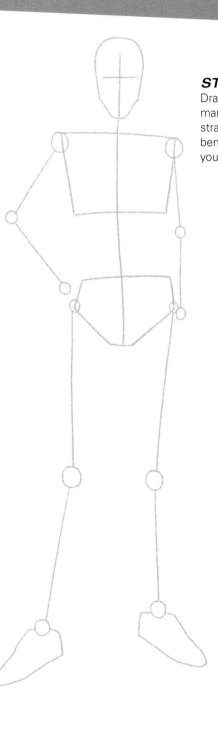

STEP 1
Draw a basic stick figure of a tall man with his left arm hanging straight down and his right arm bent at the elbow. He is looking you straight in the face.

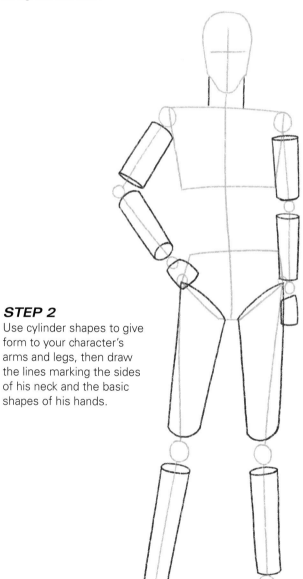

STEP 2
Use cylinder shapes to give form to your character's arms and legs, then draw the lines marking the sides of his neck and the basic shapes of his hands.

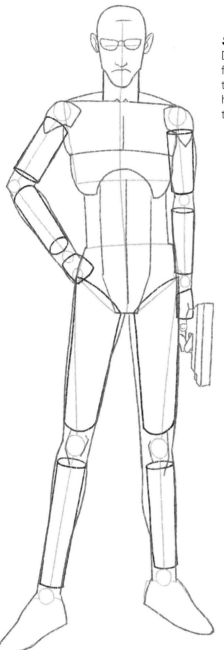

STEP 3

Draw your character's basic anatomical details and facial features. His eyes are hidden behind his glasses. Draw the gun in his left hand. The thumb and first finger of this hand are wrapped around the gun and his right hand is tucked inside his pocket.

STEP 4

Give your character some hair and eyebrows. Add details to his facial features and gun. Now it's time to draw his suit, shirt, tie, and shoes. Note how one side of his jacket is lifted up by his right arm.

STEP 5

Use your lining pen to go over the lines that will be visible in the finished drawing, and erase any pencil lines. Color the criminal's eyebrows and the sides of his hair black. Add a shadow under his chin and the creases in his suit. Draw the discarded bullet casings on the ground.

STEP 6

Put in the coloring of your character, as shown.

STEP 7

Use black and some dark colors to add shading. Use a light pen to add some highlights on his sunglasses and the edges of his suit where the light hits them.

ARTIST'S TIP

Using very sharp, straight lines for your shadows and highlights will help to make this criminal look even more angular and smart. This will reinforce the impression of him as a deadly professional.

GLOSSARY

accessories Something worn or carried as part of an outfit.

anatomical Relating to the shape of the body.

bullet casing The shell of a bullet.

cyborg A fictional person with elements from machines built into their body.

dynamic Constant change or activity.

focus lines The lines drawn around a picture to emphasize its importance.

foreshortened Made shorter than it really is, so that a picture appears to have depth.

futuristic Looking as if it is set in the future.

goggles Glasses worn to protect the eyes.

menace A threat or danger.

mimic To resemble or imitate somebody.

panel One drawing in a cartoon strip.

ribbing A structure or pattern like the ribs of a person.

FURTHER READING

How to Draw Manga Action Figures by David Antram (Book House, 2012)

Manga Now!: How to Draw Action Figures by Keith Sparrow (Search Press Ltd, 2014)

Write and Draw Your Own Comics by Louie Stowell (Usborne, 2014)

WEBSITES

Due to the changing nature of Internet links, PowerKids Press has developed an online list of websites related to the subject of this book. This site is updated regularly. Please use this link to access the list: **www.powerkidslinks.com/um/action**

INDEX